Original title:
The Frozen Echo

Copyright © 2024 Swan Charm
All rights reserved.

Author: Kaido Väinamäe
ISBN HARDBACK: 978-9916-79-549-1
ISBN PAPERBACK: 978-9916-79-550-7
ISBN EBOOK: 978-9916-79-551-4

Resonance in the Frozen Air

In the chill where echoes rest,
Whispers float, so soft, so blessed.
Frosted breath on silent trees,
Songs of winter dance with ease.

Unseen notes in icy strands,
Carry dreams across the lands.
Harmonies in crystal light,
Resonance in the quiet night.

Lullabies in Hibernation

Beneath the snow, the earth lies still,
Wrapped in dreams, a serene chill.
Nature holds its tender breath,
Lullabies of life and death.

Trees doze softly, wrapped in white,
Stars above gleam, pure and bright.
The world awaits the sun's embrace,
As dozing hearts find gentle space.

Shimmering Whispers of Winter

Crystals dance on frosted air,
Icicles hang, delicate, rare.
Whispers shimmer like the stars,
Winter's grace in silent bars.

Each flake tells a tale untold,
In the cold, the warmth unfolds.
Glimmers softly in the night,
A canvas spun with purest light.

Silence Wrapped in Snowflakes

Silence deep, like falling snow,
Hushed the world in gentle glow.
Every flake a hush profound,
Whispers soft, a magic sound.

Wrapped in layers, quiet dreams,
Nature's peace in silver seams.
Each step muffled, thoughts in flight,
Wrapped in snow, the heart feels light.

Shadows in the Shimmering White

In the glow of the winter's embrace,
Shadows dance with a delicate grace.
Whispers of frost beneath the trees,
Silent secrets carried by the breeze.

Moonlight glimmers on the icy ground,
Quiet moments where peace is found.
Footsteps muffled in a soft white layer,
Each step forward is a whispered prayer.

Snowflakes twirl like dreams in the night,
Drifting softly, a beautiful sight.
Echoes linger in the crisp, cold air,
A fleeting magic, an ephemeral flare.

The world transforms in the stillness profound,
Nature's canvas in silence renowned.
With hearts aglow in the frosty light,
We find our solace in shadows so bright.

Beneath the stars, where the wild whispers play,
We find our way through night and day.
In shimmering white, we find a home,
A world of wonder where we freely roam.

Echoed Footprints of Wintry Days

In mornings crisp with a soft golden hue,
Echoes of footsteps in the fresh, fallen dew.
Each step a story of journeys begun,
In the dance of the snow, we are all one.

Frost-kissed branches sway in the breeze,
Holding memories of long-lost leaves.
The air is sweet with a scent of pine,
Whispers of winter in this season divine.

Silent pathways beckon with allure,
Every corner turned feels so pure.
As shadows stretch beneath the fading sun,
We wander onward, two become one.

The night embraces with a starry cloak,
Glistening softly as the cold winds soak.
In the quiet, our laughter we share,
Footprints in the snow, love laid bare.

As twilight falls and the day takes flight,
We trace our paths in the pale moonlight.
Together forever, on this we agree,
Echoed footprints in wintry glee.

Echoes in the Winter Veil

Whispers drift through the cold,
Silent tales of days of old.
Frosty kisses on the air,
Nature's hush, a gentle care.

Among the trees, shadows play,
Memories of light decay.
Softly wrapped in winter's shroud,
Echoes dance, though quiet, loud.

Crystals form on barren ground,
In stillness, life is profound.
Every flake, a story spun,
Underneath the barren sun.

With each breath, the world stands still,
An endless pause, a timeless thrill.
Winter's breath, a subtle art,
Carving dreams in nature's heart.

As night descends, the stars align,
A tapestry of frost divine.
In the veil, we find our peace,
Echoes whisper, sorrows cease.

Soft Footfalls on Icy Paths

Step by step on glistening trails,
Footfalls soft, the silence hails.
Every crunch in snowy guise,
A moment caught that softly cries.

Beneath the moon's pale, watchful gaze,
Wandering lost in winter's maze.
Frosty breath, a fleeting ghost,
Chasing dreams where shadows boast.

Pine trees bow, their branches bent,
Guardians of this soft lament.
In their arms, the world feels light,
Wrapped in whispers of the night.

Gentle echoes of nature's song,
Guide us where we all belong.
With each step, the heart will soar,
Finding magic, evermore.

In the stillness of the night,
Every star, a spark of light.
Soft footfalls, a silent prayer,
In the cold, we shed our care.

Glimmers of Hope in Frozen Realms

Amidst the white, a promise gleams,
In frosted air, we chase our dreams.
Hope ignites in winter's chill,
In frozen realms, our hearts fulfill.

Golden rays pierce the grey mist,
Whispers of warmth that can't be missed.
Each dawn brings a vibrant hue,
Painting shadows with shades anew.

Through the frost, a pathway glows,
Carving life where the cold wind blows.
Nature hums a vibrant tune,
Beneath the watchful winter moon.

In crystal hearts, the future wakes,
Glimmers shine with every flake.
Resilient spirit in the cold,
Strength is woven in tales told.

With each heartbeat, hope unfolds,
In silent woods, the truth that holds.
Glimmers of joy in frozen lands,
Embrace us tightly with gentle hands.

Snowbound Shadows Break the Silence

Silent whispers in the night,
Soft shadows dance, a fleeting sight.
Snowbound visions, fleeting grace,
In the stillness, we find our place.

Each flake falls like a sigh,
Blanketing earth, as time slips by.
The world is hushed, an embrace tight,
Wrapped in dreams, both dark and light.

Footprints map the snowy ground,
Echoes of journeys, lost yet found.
In the silence, shadows creep,
Secrets buried, they softly seep.

Night unfolds its velvet cloak,
A canvas where the heart awoke.
The stars above begin to gleam,
Breaking stillness with a dream.

In the quiet, we find our song,
In the snow, we all belong.
Snowbound shadows, soft and bright,
Guide us gently through the night.

The Solstice Sigh

In the stillness, shadows play,
Whispers dance at end of day.
Nature sleeps, the world's in pause,
Underneath the winter's cause.

Softly glows the fading light,
Stars awaken, hearts take flight.
Time stands still, a gentle sigh,
The solstice holds a secret high.

Frosted leaves on branches cling,
Softly now, the nightbirds sing.
Luminous dreams of warmth return,
In our hearts, a quiet burn.

As the world drifts into night,
Echoes linger, pure delight.
In the dark, we find our way,
Guided by the moon's soft ray.

Embers glow in fireside cheer,
Gathered close, our loved ones near.
In this moment, calm and bright,
We embrace the longest night.

Echoes of a Winter's Past

Memories wrapped in silver frost,
Whispers of what was once lost.
Laughter echoes through the trees,
Carried softly by the breeze.

Footprints left in fallen snow,
Tell a tale of long ago.
Each soft flake a story spun,
Underneath the pale, cold sun.

Blankets woven from the night,
Shield us from the coming light.
Chilled fingers, warm hearts collide,
As we gather side by side.

The fireplace crackles, flames arise,
Casting shadows, warming sighs.
In the quiet, time stands still,
Echoes dance upon the chill.

Winter nights, a sweet embrace,
Hold us close in their soft grace.
In the quiet, hear the past,
As the cold winds whisper fast.

Murmurs Beneath the Snow

Beneath the blanket, life does breathe,
Silent whispers, nature weaves.
In the stillness, secrets lie,
Waiting for the spring to try.

Each fallen flake, a tale concealed,
Underneath, the earth revealed.
Roots entwined in winter's grip,
Holding fast their dormant trip.

As the thaw begins to tease,
Awakening beneath the trees.
Murmurs rise from slumber's hold,
Stories of the brave and bold.

In the hush, the world prepares,
For the sun's warm, golden flares.
Every heartbeat, every sigh,
Pushes forth to meet the sky.

Life emerges, bright and new,
Chasing shadows, breaking through.
Murmurs soft, a gentle sound,
Winter's grasp released, unbound.

Frosted Memories in Twilight

Twilight drapes in icy veils,
Casting down its chilly trails.
Shadows stretch and whispers blend,
As the day begins to end.

Frosted memories linger sweet,
In the quiet, hearts do meet.
Golden hues of fleeting light,
Guide us gently into night.

Snowflakes fall like dreams untold,
Each unique, a story bold.
In their dance, the silence grows,
Wrapped in twilight's softest throes.

Glistening branches, stars align,
Nature's canvas, pure and fine.
In the dusk, we find our peace,
As the frigid whispers cease.

Frosted ground beneath our feet,
Echoes fade, but hearts still beat.
In the twilight, memories sway,
Forever dance, forever stay.

Traces Lost in the Freeze

Footprints vanish in the snow,
Time weaves whispers soft and low.
Ghosts of laughter in the breeze,
Shadows dance beneath the trees.

Icicles drip like melting dreams,
Frozen stillness holds its schemes.
A world wrapped in winter's cloak,
Silent echoes where we spoke.

Frosted branches, crystal bright,
Every gaze a fleeting light.
Chill of longing in the air,
Memories linger everywhere.

Beneath the surface, warmth resides,
In the depths where hope abides.
Time will break the morning's greed,
As sunflowers bloom from winter's seed.

Yet for now, we stand apart,
Hearing whispers in the heart.
Traces lost in the freeze,
Awaiting spring's gentle tease.

Whispers in a Crystal Chamber

In chambers echoing with frost,
Every breath a word embossed.
Crystal silence wraps us tight,
Whispers woven in the night.

Moonlight spills on icy sheen,
Soft reflections, quiet scene.
Voices drift on frosted air,
Forgotten tales linger there.

Shadows pulse with secrets old,
Crystalline stories yet untold.
In this chamber, dreams conspire,
Frozen thoughts that never tire.

Whispers dance on silver beams,
Gentle music, frozen dreams.
Embers glowing in the cold,
Intimate moments to behold.

Breathe the stillness, pause the hour,
In the crystal, find your power.
Whispers linger, sweet embrace,
In this chamber, time and space.

Silent Glimpses of Winter's Heart

Snowflakes drift like gentle sighs,
Painting tales across gray skies.
Silent glimpses, soft and clear,
Winter's heart draws ever near.

Branches laden, heavy, white,
Whispers wrapped in bitter night.
Each flake a story formed in flight,
Captured in the fading light.

Crimson berries clutch the leaves,
Hushed beneath the gathering eaves.
Nature pauses, breath held tight,
In the silence, pure delight.

Fields are blanketed in peace,
All the world seems to release.
Ghostly echoes of the dawn,
Winter's magic lingers on.

As frost weaves patterns on the ground,
In every whisper, life is found.
Silent moments, winter's art,
Glimpses deep within the heart.

Fragments of a Shattered Chill

Shattered echoes in the night,
Fragments of a fleeting light.
Chill that settles in the bones,
Winter sings in shattered tones.

Crystal shards beneath the moon,
Melodies of a frozen tune.
Stars are scattered, pale and bright,
Lost within the haze of white.

Every breath a cloud of grey,
Whispers of a long-lost day.
In the quiet, secrets spill,
Floating softly on the chill.

Time is captured in the frost,
Memories of what was lost.
Fragments in the winter's grasp,
Fleeting thoughts we long to clasp.

Nothing stays, as winter gleams,
All that lingers are our dreams.
In this freeze, we find the thrill,
Precious moments held until.

A Song of Silent Icicles

In the hush of winter's night,
Icicles cling, pure and bright.
Whispers echo through the trees,
Silent songs in the cold breeze.

Frozen tears on window panes,
Nature's beauty softly reigns.
Glistening under pale moonlight,
A fragile world, serene and white.

Each drop dances to the ground,
In the quiet, peace is found.
Chilling winds that gently sigh,
Carry secrets, low and high.

Branches bow in frosty grace,
Time stands still in this embrace.
Icicles like crystal spears,
Guard the silence through the years.

Winter's breath, a soft refrain,
Echoing like a distant train.
In this realm, no sounds collide,
Just the faith of winter's glide.

Breath of a Snowbound Silence

Snowflakes dance in the still air,
Whispers of winter everywhere.
The world wrapped in a blanket white,
A serene, captivating sight.

Footsteps vanish, soft and slow,
In the realm where cold winds blow.
Trees adorned in shimmering frost,
In this moment, nothing is lost.

The hush of snowflakes as they fall,
Nature's quiet, a tranquil call.
Breath held tight in the frozen land,
Underneath this frosty band.

A gentle murmur of the night,
Stars above, a glimmering light.
In the depth of winter's grace,
Silence dances, fills the space.

As shadows stretch and twilight fades,
In the peace, time slowly wades.
A breath of calm, a gentle sigh,
In snowbound silence, we lie.

The Glacial Resound

From frozen depths, a sound does rise,
Echoing through the vast, blue skies.
Glaciers groan, their stories told,
In icy breath, both fierce and bold.

Each crack resonates with the past,
A symphony, a spell is cast.
Waves of chill in the evening air,
Nature's heartbeat, both harsh and rare.

Frosted whispers mingle and weave,
In the silence, we believe.
Beneath the ice, life stirs anew,
Hidden wonders, a world in view.

The dance of frost, a timeless play,
Guiding the night into the day.
Join the chorus, feel it deep,
In glacial resound, secrets keep.

Time slows down in this vast expanse,
Where echoes weave their ancient dance.
Resounding through the cosmos wide,
In the chill, all dreams abide.

Remnants of a Frosty Serenade

Beneath the moonlight's gentle glow,
Frosty tendrils twist and flow.
A serenade of winter's cheer,
Whispers soft, for all to hear.

Icicles drip in rhythmic beat,
Nature's music, pure and sweet.
Each note hangs in the frigid air,
A melody, both rare and fair.

Footsteps crunch on powdery trails,
Stories carried on the gales.
Remnants of the day now fade,
In the night, a new serenade.

Snowflakes glide, a silent flight,
Kissing earth, a swirl of white.
Softly, the world falls into dreams,
Under the moon's silvery beams.

The night embraces, wrapped in cold,
A tale of winter gently told.
In frosty serenade, we find,
A thread of peace in heart and mind.

Murmurs of Icebound Dreams

In the stillness, shadows glow,
Whispers of the night drift slow.
Crystals caught in twilight's gleam,
Frozen paths of a fragile dream.

Stars are distant, hopes alight,
Pathways winding, veiled in white.
Voices carried on the breeze,
Secrets shared among the trees.

Silent wishes softly weave,
Through the frost, they dance and leave.
Echoes of what might have been,
In the chill, lost moments spin.

Beneath the blanket, worlds are spun,
Frosted tales of moon and sun.
Laughter lingers, fleeting weight,
In the ice, we find our fate.

So let the whispers guide our way,
In this realm where dreams play.
Murmurs weave through the night's seam,
In the heart of icebound dream.

Echoes in the Frost

Footprints fade in silent snow,
Softly speaking as we go.
Each step marks a fleeting trace,
In the frost, time finds its place.

Shadows dance upon the white,
Echoes of the day take flight.
Sculpted forms in crystal glow,
Memories where the cold winds blow.

Breath of winter, crisp and clear,
Whispers held for all to hear.
Voices linger, faint yet near,
In the frost, our dreams are sheer.

Every glimmer, every spark,
Holds a story in the dark.
Echoes echo, loud and soft,
Finding warmth in snowy lofts.

As night deepens, stars ignite,
Guiding us through winter's night.
Each echo, a gentle call,
In the frost, we rise and fall.

Frigid Reflections

In mirrors made of icy glass,
Silent stories slowly pass.
Glimpses of what we once knew,
Frigid dreams in chilling hue.

Every tear a jewel bright,
Caught within the frozen light.
Thoughts of warmth, a distant thing,
In this cold, our hearts still sing.

Ripples dance on silver streams,
Holding fragments of lost dreams.
Nature's canvas, stark and bare,
Frigid whispers fill the air.

Clouds of silver, skies so grey,
Frigid visions lead the way.
Winter's breath, a fleeting touch,
In reflections, we feel so much.

As mornings break, we find our grace,
In frozen realms, we find our place.
Frigid echoes gently chime,
In reflections, we freeze time.

Soundwaves of the Snow

Snowflakes drift on whispers light,
Blanketing the world in white.
Each flake carries a silent tune,
Playing softly 'neath the moon.

In the hush, vibrations soar,
Soundwaves dancing at the core.
Nature's symphony unfolds,
In the chill, the magic holds.

Winter's breath, a soft embrace,
Filling every tranquil space.
Echoes travel through the frost,
In this silence, nothing's lost.

Heartbeat resonates in air,
Melding with the frosty stare.
Every crunch a rhythmic beat,
In the snow, we find our feet.

Let the soundwaves guide us near,
In this realm of chills we steer.
Songs of winter, pure and low,
In the silence of the snow.

Frosty Nothings

Beneath the frost, silence sleeps,
Whispers of dreams, in snowdrifts deep.
Footprints fade, as winter sighs,
A world concealed beneath pale skies.

Crystals sparkle, hearts grow cold,
Each breath a story, yet untold.
In the stillness, shadows play,
Time drifts on, like snowflakes stray.

Branches bow with heavy grace,
Nature's art in frozen space.
Hopes may linger in the chill,
Yet warmth resides in heart and will.

Whimsical Whispers

In the wind, soft secrets dance,
Laughter twirls, a playful chance.
Clouds decorate a sunlit sky,
Imagination learns to fly.

Dreams flutter like butterflies,
Between goodbyes and sweet goodbyes.
Each thought a spark, a gentle glow,
Where wishes wander, breezes blow.

Stars blink down with knowing smiles,
Guiding hearts across the miles.
In this moment, we unite,
Whispers weave through day and night.

Resilience Beneath the Thaw

Beneath the ice, life stirs anew,
Roots embrace the earth's warm hue.
Tiny buds break through the frost,
In every ending, beauty's lost.

Hope rises with the morning sun,
A quiet battle just begun.
Life pulses strong in hidden veins,
Defiant against the winter's chains.

With every drop of melting snow,
The promise of spring begins to grow.
Wonders wait in patience near,
Resilience whispers in our ear.

Murmurs of Immemorial Cold

Whispers echo through the night,
Ancient stories take their flight.
Time's embrace, a chilling breath,
Lessons learned from shadows of death.

In ice-bound fields, echoes sing,
Of seasons lost, and the pain they bring.
Yet in the sorrow, wisdom hides,
Knowledge rests where stillness bides.

Frozen hearts, yet they can feel,
A path to love that pain can heal.
Through cold embraces, life persists,
In the silence, a hope exists.

Chilling Conversations in the Silence

Between the trees, the silence speaks,
In frost-kissed branches, stillness seeks.
Whispers carried on a breeze,
Nature's tales, the wandering freeze.

Conversations wrapped in snow,
Each flake, a part of all we know.
Hearts listen to the quiet call,
In the hush, we rise or fall.

Echoes linger, soft yet bold,
Chilling words that never grow old.
In the silence, truths unfold,
Winter's heart, a story told.

Shimmering Glaciers

Beneath a sky of timeless blue,
The glaciers gleam, a wondrous view.
With hues of white and hints of grey,
Their silent beauty holds at bay.

Time carves its art on icy plains,
Where whispers ride the chilly rains.
The sun reflects on frozen dreams,
In dazzling light, the silence beams.

Each crevice tells a tale untold,
Of ancient worlds and secrets cold.
The winds that sing through frosty nights,
Carry the songs of winter's rites.

With every crack, a thunderous sound,
Nature's pulse in silence found.
The shimmering surface quivers bright,
A dance of shadows and soft light.

In winter's grasp, they stand so tall,
Guardians of the land, they call.
In their embrace, the world stands still,
As time drifts slow, against its will.

Celestial Frost

Under the moon's pale, glowing gaze,
A fine frost weaves in a silver haze.
Each blade of grass, a crystal gem,
Nature's artwork, a delicate hymn.

Stars above in a velvet night,
Twinkle softly, a shimmering light.
They whisper secrets through the chill,
In every sparkle, time stands still.

The air is crisp, a breath of peace,
In winter's grasp, all worries cease.
With each exhale, a cloud of white,
A fleeting moment, pure delight.

The world transformed by nature's hand,
A frosty blanket on the land.
It wraps the earth in tranquil grace,
A fleeting kiss from winter's face.

As dawn arrives with hues of gold,
The frost retreats, the tales unfold.
Yet in our hearts, the chill remains,
A memory of frozen chains.

A Chill in the Air

When autumn leaves begin to fall,
A whispering breeze begins to call.
A chill creeps in, a soft embrace,
The season shifts, it leaves its trace.

Bare branches stretch against the sky,
As clouds roll in, the winds sigh high.
The air turns crisp, a fleeting thrill,
Nature's breath, both calm and still.

A shiver runs down weary spines,
As daylight wanes, the moon aligns.
The stars emerge in frosty night,
A tapestry of silver light.

Each step through crunching frosted ground,
Echoes softly, a soothing sound.
The chill invites, it draws us near,
Embrace the cold, shed every fear.

For in the frost, there's beauty rare,
In every sigh, in every hair.
A chill in the air reminds us true,
Life's fleeting moments, a precious view.

Hushed Voices of the Snow

In the stillness of falling snow,
Hushed voices speak, a gentle flow.
Each flake a whisper from above,
A soft embrace, a tale of love.

They blanket earth in purest white,
Transforming all into pure delight.
With every flake, a secret sent,
In silence deep, the world is lent.

Footsteps muffled, a sacred sound,
The snowy hush wraps all around.
Nature pauses and takes a breath,
In winter's arms, it dances with death.

The trees adorned in crystal lace,
Stand as sentinels, calm and grace.
They sway softly, as breezes sigh,
In winter's realm, the dreams don't die.

For in this quiet, magic lives,
As snow bestows what nature gives.
Hushed voices linger on the breeze,
In every drift, there lies a tease.

When Frost Adorns the Silence

Morning glimmers with icy grace,
Frosty whispers embrace each space.
Nature holds its breath so still,
Wrapped in winter's frosted will.

Branches wear a crystal crown,
Glistening softly, never brown.
Footprints trace where spirits tread,
In the quiet, peace is spread.

Echoes of a world asleep,
Secrets that the cold winds keep.
Hearts beat softly, dreams take flight,
In the hush of fading light.

Snowflakes dance in sweet delight,
Twinkling softly, pure and bright.
Each a story, unique and neat,
Carpet laid beneath our feet.

As stars emerge, the sky is clear,
Frigid air, a whispered cheer.
Nature's canvas, white and vast,
A fleeting beauty, dimming fast.

Haunting Harmonies of the Frozen

Wind caresses the barren trees,
Nature sings with frozen ease.
Notes of silence, soft and low,
Echoes through the falling snow.

Each flake carries a secret sound,
In the stillness, magic found.
Voices swirl like snowflakes' flight,
In the shadows of the night.

Moonlight bathes the world below,
Illuminating silver glow.
Melodies of frost entwined,
Awaken dreams that lingered blind.

Whispers rising from the frost,
In this realm, no moment's lost.
Haunting harmonies ring clear,
Calling spirits, drawing near.

As dawn breaks with gentle light,
Frosty tunes fade out of sight.
Yet the echoes softly dwell,
In the hearts we cannot tell.

Dreaming in a Snowy Abode

Within the walls, a fire glows,
Outside rests where the cold wind blows.
Blankets woven with stories warm,
Embrace us safe from winter's storm.

Windows framed with frosty lace,
Whispers dance in a cozy space.
In the night, as shadows creep,
Dreams are sown in tranquil sleep.

Footsteps muffled, muted sighs,
Crackling wood and starlit skies.
Through the panes, the world lies tight,
Wrapped in flurries, pure and white.

Each soft breath a gentle song,
In this haven, we belong.
Hot cocoa warms our hands and hearts,
As winter's magic slowly starts.

With every flake that tumbles down,
Hope unfurls in frosted gown.
In snowy dreams, we find our peace,
As winter's grip brings sweet release.

Chimes of the Winter Wind

Listen close to whispers low,
Chimes of winter softly flow.
Through the branches, a soft song,
Notes of frost where we belong.

Each breath carried on the breeze,
Dances lightly among the trees.
Echoes weave through twilight's glow,
In the chill, a warmth will grow.

Winds that shuffle through the night,
Calling dreams in silver light.
Nature hums a haunting tune,
Beneath the watchful, glowing moon.

From the rooftops, soft and clear,
Melodies that we hold dear.
Through the hush, the melodies shine,
Chimes of winter, yours and mine.

As dawn breaks with painted skies,
Resonance of love replies.
In the air, sweet notes ascend,
With the wind, our hearts blend.

Chilled Chords of Memory

In whispers soft, the echoes play,
Notes of past drift far away.
Each melody, a ghostly thread,
Binding dreams of what was said.

Frosted thoughts in twilight's glow,
Memories like embers flow.
Chilled winds carry tales so dear,
For in these chords, the heart draws near.

Time's embrace, a tender sigh,
Holding close what won't say goodbye.
Songs of yore in silence weave,
Ghosts of longing, we believe.

Fractured notes beneath the ice,
Whispers threaded, soft and nice.
Chilled chords ring with every beat,
A symphony of lost retreat.

In shadows deep, where echoes blend,
Timeless tunes that never end.
With every breath, the music flows,
Chilled chords where the heart still knows.

The Stillness of Sound

In the quiet, whispers dwell,
Softly ringing like a bell.
A gentle pause, the world unfolds,
In stillness, every story holds.

The silence wraps in a warm embrace,
Time stands still, a tranquil space.
Each heartbeat echoes in the night,
A symphony of pure delight.

Beneath the stars, the world sleeps on,
Dreams awaken with the dawn.
A hush that tells of moments past,
The stillness holds, forever cast.

In every corner, quiet reigns,
Peaceful moments, no more chains.
The stillness of sound, a balm so sweet,
Inviting whispers, soft retreat.

Listen close and you will find,
Harmony within the mind.
In frozen breath, the music calls,
The stillness of sound within us all.

Frozen Footprints

A path untold in glistening white,
Footprints lead into the night.
Each step whispers tales of yore,
Frozen dreams on a silent shore.

In snow-kissed lands where shadows play,
We wander lost, then find our way.
Footprints fade, as time moves fast,
Footprints linger, but never last.

Each mark we leave, a story spun,
In winter's grasp, we come undone.
A journey brief, yet ever deep,
Frozen memories, secrets we keep.

The chill surrounds, a blanket low,
Covering paths we used to know.
A dance of echoes where we tread,
Footprints whisper what we dread.

Yet in this frost, a warmth we find,
The heart's true map, forever kind.
Though footprints fade, we carry on,
In frozen paths, our souls have drawn.

Resonance of the Cold

In icy realms where silence reigns,
A sharpness felt through body gains.
Each breath released, a cloud of gray,
Resonates the cold's ballet.

Harmony found in frosted air,
Notes of chill spin everywhere.
Winter's song, a gentle plea,
Echoes through the frozen tree.

In crystal shards, the music's cast,
Resonance whispers, echoes vast.
Beneath the frost, a pulse so bold,
The heart dances in the cold.

Every flake a silent sound,
In the stillness, life is found.
A symphony where shadows creep,
Resonance of the cold, we keep.

As daybreak casts its golden rays,
The resonance shifts and gently sways.
Yet in the heart, the cold remains,
In winter's touch, our spirit gains.

Frostbitten Fantasies

In twilight's grasp, the cold winds sigh,
Dreams linger where the shadows lie.
Whispers soft as the falling frost,
In a world where warmth is lost.

Glistening branches, a silver lace,
Memories frozen in time and space.
Each breath of air, a crystal shard,
Hearts wrapped tight, forever scarred.

Underneath a blanket of white,
Stars twinkle like gems in the night.
Wandering souls, we seek, we pine,
For a moment when love was divine.

Footprints fade on the icy ground,
Echoes of laughter, a distant sound.
Through the silence, we start to see,
Frostbitten dreams that long to be free.

In the stillness, a dream takes flight,
An ember's glow ignites the night.
With hope entwined in every breath,
We dance on the edge of life and death.

Chilling Reveries

Beneath the moon's pale, ghostly glow,
Chilling winds begin to blow.
In shadows deep, our secrets dwell,
Wrapped in frost, a silent spell.

Snowflakes whisper tales of old,
Frozen stories waiting to be told.
Each drift hides a lingering sigh,
Memories masked as time drifts by.

Hushed moments brush the quiet ground,
In the stillness, lost dreams abound.
A tapestry woven with icy thread,
Crafting paths that we once tread.

Crystals form where feelings freeze,
In the air hangs a breath of ease.
Through the cold, hope glimmers bright,
In chilling reveries of the night.

The heart remembers, though lips grow numb,
Yearning for warmth, it quietly hums.
Tales of love, in frost laid bare,
Chilling echoes linger in the air.

Silence Between the Snowflakes

In the hush between each flake,
Time suspends with every shake.
A world transformed, both soft and bright,
Clad in garments of purest white.

The silence sings, a soothing tune,
Beneath the watchful, silver moon.
In this quiet, hearts collide,
Secrets held, nowhere to hide.

Crimson berries against the frost,
Bright gems of warmth, never lost.
Each step a whisper on the ground,
A ballet of silence all around.

Glimmers catch in the waning light,
Breathless beauty ignites the night.
In the stillness, souls can mend,
Finding peace where pathways blend.

Between the snowflakes, a promise lies,
Dancing softly beneath the skies.
In this space where dreams awake,
We find our truth, the silence breaks.

A Song of Ice and Memory

Frozen veins in the chill of dawn,
Echoes of laughter, now nearly gone.
Each crystal holds a story near,
A song of ice that we must hear.

Through misty breaths, reminders fall,
Memories linger, a haunting call.
In whispers soft, the past returns,
A flicker of flame in the heart that yearns.

Waves of white on the frozen ground,
In their embrace, lost hopes are found.
Dance of shadows, flicker of light,
In silence embraced by the night.

As winter's grip begins to lift,
Time unfolds every cherished gift.
Though ice may reign in the darkest days,
Love endures in myriad ways.

A melody weaved through frost and snow,
In each refrain, memories grow.
With hearts entwined, we will remember,
A song of ice, a glowing ember.

Crystals of Distant Lullabies

Gentle whispers float on air,
Echoes of dreams that softly share.
Each note a sparkle, pure and bright,
Guiding lost souls through the night.

In twilight's grasp, they intertwine,
Crystals glimmer, a soft divine.
Carrying hope from afar,
Lighting paths like a distant star.

Nights adorned with silver tones,
Cradling hearts in tender moans.
Melodies that drift and sway,
In the quiet, where shadows play.

With every breath, a lullaby,
Cascading under the velvet sky.
A chorus of dreams, serene yet wild,
Embracing the world, gentle and mild.

So let the crystals shine anew,
As distant lullabies still ring true.
In their glow, we find our peace,
As all our worries slowly cease.

When Time Stands Still in Frost

Frozen moments hold their breath,
Beneath the skies, a quiet death.
Time's embrace, a gentle freeze,
Whispers linger on the breeze.

Crystals form on every tree,
Nature's art for all to see.
Stillness reigns in wintry gold,
A tale of silence now retold.

Footsteps echo on the ground,
Lost in beauty all around.
Each step a careful, measured dance,
Caught in nature's frosty glance.

Stars above in stillness gleam,
In this moment, we can dream.
When time suspends its steady flow,
The world transforms; all hearts grow slow.

In winter's grasp, we seek the light,
A promise held in the cold night.
For in the hush, we find our way,
When time stands still, forever stay.

Chilling Reverberations in Shadows

In the dark, the echoes roam,
Whispers that feel so far from home.
Shadows dancing in their fright,
Chilling reverberations ignite.

Fingers trace the edges bold,
Secrets hiding, tales untold.
A canvas painted with despair,
Softly woven in the air.

Creeping doubts, they intertwine,
Shattering peace like aged wine.
Through the gloom, a voice calls still,
In the night, where hearts can chill.

Cold winds speak of things unkind,
Haunting echoes in the mind.
Yet within shadows lies a spark,
Where healing whispers pierce the dark.

So let the chilly tones resound,
In the stillness, beauty's found.
For though the night may seem so vast,
Hope lives on, free from the past.

Eclipsed Dreams in Icebound Realms

In realms where silence reigns supreme,
Eclipsed dreams form in every beam.
Icebound visions, frozen tight,
Glimmers caught in the pale moonlight.

Fragmented wishes, lost in time,
Songs of sorrow mixed with rhyme.
Bound by frost, yet they persist,
Daring souls to still exist.

Crystals dance in cosmic play,
In the heart where shadows sway.
Echoes of the dreams once bright,
Now wrapped in the icy night.

Beneath the weight of cold despair,
Lingers hope, a breath of air.
For in the depth, a flicker glows,
A path to warmth where love still flows.

So let our dreams thaw in the light,
Forged anew, a stunning sight.
In icebound realms, we'll find our way,
As eclipsed dreams greet the day.

Frosted Tales from Forgotten Woods

Whispers of the trees so tall,
Frosted branches gently fall.
Echoes of laughter, long since gone,
Beneath a sky of fading dawn.

A tale of old, wrapped in white,
Footprints hidden, lost from sight.
Moonlight dances on the snow,
Bringing warmth to hearts below.

Secrets linger through the night,
In the glow of silver light.
Every flake, a story spun,
In this land where dreams do run.

Timber frames and frozen streams,
Cradle softly whispered dreams.
Nature's breath, a silent sigh,
In the woods where memories lie.

So let us wander, hand in hand,
Through this frosted, timeless land.
For in the tales of old we find,
The magic of a wandering mind.

Echoing Footsteps in the Snow

Silent night, a world anew,
Blankets soft in powdery hue.
Footsteps crunch on frosty ground,
As whispers of the night abound.

Stars above, like diamonds shine,
Lighting paths where hearts entwine.
Cold winds sing a haunting tune,
Beneath the watchful, silver moon.

Echoes call from distant trees,
Bridging gaps on winter's breeze.
Each breath a cloud, each glance a prayer,
In stillness wrapped, we find our care.

Wandering through this frozen maze,
Lost in thoughts of yesterdays.
Time stands still, yet moves so fast,
In snowy realms where shadows cast.

Through the silence, stories weave,
In the night, we dare believe.
With every step, a bond we sow,
Echoing softly in the snow.

Chilled Notes of a Frozen Ballad

Frosty air and icy strands,
Nature's chorus gently stands.
Every note a crystal clear,
ringing softly through the year.

Underneath the starry skies,
Melodies float, like whispered sighs.
Voices quiet, but alive,
In this magic, we shall thrive.

Snowflakes twirl in waltzing grace,
Carrying dreams from place to place.
Notes collide, a harmony,
Frozen ballads wild and free.

As the world drapes in white lace,
We find warmth in this sacred space.
Chilled arias weave through the night,
Painting shadows in their flight.

Songs of winter fill the air,
Binding souls in tender care.
Together we shall softly hum,
Chilled notes of a frostbitten drum.

Melodies of the Icebound Soul

In the silence, whispers grow,
Songs of winter, soft and slow.
Icebound spirits find their song,
In the void, where we belong.

Frigid winds, they carry tales,
Of distant lands and snowy trails.
Heartbeats echo in the chill,
As time stands still on every hill.

Winding paths, a frosty dance,
Beneath this sky, a fleeting glance.
Each moment sings of love and strife,
Melodies of our frozen life.

Through the woods, we roam in grace,
Finding warmth in this embrace.
With every note, we break the mold,
Icebound souls, forever bold.

Together we shall sing our truth,
Echoing echoes of our youth.
In this winter, hearts unroll,
Embracing deeply the icebound soul.

A Symphony of Stillness

In silence, whispers float through air,
Gentle breezes, free from despair.
Trees sway lightly, leaves shiver bright,
Wrapped in shadows, kissed by night.

Stars above play their distant tune,
Eyes closed softly, cradled by moon.
Nature hums in a tranquil key,
A symphony of serenity.

Softly falls the gentle dew,
Kissing petals, fresh and new.
Echoes linger, time stands still,
Quietude grips, a perfect thrill.

Mountains hold the secrets tight,
Guarding dreams till dawn's first light.
In each moment, peace unwinds,
A symphony for restless minds.

Awakening the heart's soft song,
In stillness, we find we belong.
Harmony flows, a river wide,
In silence, let the soul abide.

Enigmas Wrapped in Frost

Morning glimmers, a world ensnared,
Frosted whispers, highly prepared.
Nature's secrets, held tight in ice,
Mysteries linger, soft and precise.

Brittle branches, adorned with white,
Shade the ground, pure and bright.
Every breath a cloud of dreams,
Reality mutters while still it seems.

Crystals sparkle in sunlight's gaze,
Time transforms in winter's haze.
Silent echoes in the frozen air,
Enigmas dance with elegant flair.

Footsteps crunch on a blanket dense,
Every step speaks, a silent repentance.
The world shivers, secrets unfold,
In winter's embrace, life tells the bold.

Frozen currents beneath the skin,
Mysteries wait for magic to begin.
Wrapped in frost, the heart beats slow,
Carrying tales of ages ago.

The Lull of Frozen Twilight

As twilight falls, the world exhales,
Shadows stretch where daylight pales.
A hush blankets the sleeping land,
In twilight's hold, all dreams stand.

Colors dim in the fading light,
Whispers weave through the cooling night.
Time pauses, a gentle sigh,
Underneath the wide, starry sky.

Snow blankets the earth like a shroud,
A serene silence, beautifully loud.
Nature rests, cradled in the hush,
Embraced in twilight's softening blush.

Moonlight glimmers on icy streams,
Reflecting back our deepest dreams.
In the stillness, hearts begin to mend,
With each breath, the night descends.

Underneath this twilight's glow,
The world whispers secrets we long to know.
In frozen beauty, dreams delight,
In the lull of this quiet night.

Prism of the Crystal Whisper

A prism forms in dawn's embrace,
Reflecting light with gentle grace.
Crystal whispers dance on air,
Flashes of color, bright and rare.

Sunlight filters through the trees,
Painting moments, time's soft tease.
Each droplet gleams, a fleeting spark,
In nature's canvas, shadows stark.

Dewdrops gather, a jeweled crest,
Nature's art at its very best.
In every glimmer, stories hide,
In the silence, they do abide.

Rainbows arch their vibrant wings,
As life awakens and sweetly sings.
In the prism, echoes dance and sway,
Moments linger, softly play.

Etching beauty in heart and mind,
In the whispers, our souls unwind.
Nature's gifts, forever bright,
In the crystal's fleeting light.

Whispers in Winter's Grasp

Snowflakes dance in the chilled air,
Soft whispers echo, fading rare.
Frost bites gently, a quiet plea,
Nature's hush wraps around me.

Pine trees stand, cloaked in white,
Silent sentinels, bathed in light.
Moonlight glimmers on frozen streams,
Lost in the world of winter's dreams.

Footprints trace on the glistening ground,
Every sound feels profound.
A breath escapes, mist in the cold,
Secrets of winter, softly told.

Branches bow, heavy with snow,
A tranquil beauty, soft and slow.
Winter's grasp, a gentle hold,
In whispers of silence, stories unfold.

The night wraps close, a velvet shroud,
Under stars, quiet and proud.
In winter's embrace, I find my place,
Lost in the magic, a tranquil grace.

Shards of Silence

In the stillness, echoes remain,
Fractured thoughts, a haunting refrain.
The void whispers where shadows creep,
In shards of silence, secrets seep.

Time stands still, suspended in air,
Moments linger, heavy with care.
A distant sound, the heart's gentle beat,
In silence, solitude feels complete.

The past lingers like a ghost,
Whispers of what mattered most.
Between the lines, unspoken fears,
Captured memories, soaked in tears.

Voices echo, fading away,
Lost in the twilight, shadows play.
Cracks in the silence, sharp and deep,
In the quiet, we dare to weep.

Yet in this stillness, hope can grow,
From shards of silence, new seeds sow.
A fragile peace, woven with light,
In the darkness, we find our sight.

Crystal Reverberations

In crystal halls where echoes sing,
Shattering time with each soft ring.
Reflections dance on shimmering glass,
Moments captured, fleeting pass.

A prism's glow, colors collide,
Radiant whispers that cannot hide.
Through the air, like a gentle breeze,
Reverberations bring me to my knees.

Every note, a story told,
In crystal laughter, bold yet cold.
In the stillness, a chorus forms,
A symphony of silent storms.

The heart beats strong in this space,
In echoes of joy, I find my grace.
A harmony that transcends time,
In crystal reverberations, I climb.

Closing my eyes, I breathe it in,
A tranquil dance, where dreams begin.
In the essence of sound, I reside,
In the crystal chamber, wide and bright.

Glacial Harmonies

Icebergs drift on a restless sea,
In glacial harmonies, wild and free.
The ocean breathes a timeless song,
In this frozen world, we all belong.

Waves crash softly against the shore,
Whispers of ancients, tales of yore.
A symphony played by nature's hand,
In glacial beauty, we understand.

Every fracture tells a story bright,
Painting dreams in shades of light.
Melodies blend in the crisp, cold air,
Echoing softly, a melody rare.

Frosty winds weave through the trees,
A chill that sends shivers and frees.
In each note, the world stands still,
Glacial harmonies, the soul they fill.

As twilight falls, a canvas vast,
The night embraces the day that passed.
In this frozen refrain, I find my peace,
In glacial harmonies, all worries cease.

Echoes through Frost-laden Branches

In the stillness of the night,
Whispers wrap the trees so tight.
Frost-laden branches bow and sway,
Silent secrets drift away.

Moonlit paths of silver sheen,
Nature's song is soft, serene.
Echoes linger on the breeze,
Dancing through the bending leaves.

Footsteps crunch on frozen ground,
In this hush, magic is found.
Every sigh of winter's breath,
Speaks of life amidst the death.

Stars like diamonds start to gleam,
Lighting up the tranquil stream.
Frosty patterns weave and flow,
Painting tales of winter's glow.

As dawn awakens all around,
Colors burst without a sound.
In the echoes, hearts take flight,
Through frost-laden branches' night.

Quietude in the Winter Blossom

Amidst the snow, a flower blooms,
Embraced by winter, nature's womb.
Petals soft, yet brave they stand,
Whispers of the sunrays' hand.

Silent gardens wrapped in white,
Glimmers spark in morning light.
Winter's touch on fragile lace,
Holds beauty in its cold embrace.

Crystalline petals, pure and bright,
Reflecting dreams of warmer nights.
Each pause, a promise gently woven,
In quietude, all hearts are chosen.

With every snowfall, strength is born,
A cycle of life, each day is sworn.
Winter blossoms rise anew,
In their stillness, hope breaks through.

So let the world embrace this scene,
In winter's arms, the heart is keen.
For every frozen breath we take,
A quiet soul may gently wake.

Chilling Captures of Frozen Light

Icicles hang like crystal spears,
Glistening bright through winter years.
Each prism caught in frosty air,
Reflects the magic lurking there.

Lakes transformed to mirrors clear,
Chilling captures, nature's cheer.
Every shard reflects a dream,
Frozen moments, time's soft scheme.

Footprints trace a silent path,
In the cold, we find our math.
Counting stars that dance above,
As the frigid night unfolds love.

Colors muted, whispers soft,
In stillness, heartbeats drift aloft.
From every shadow, light behold,
Chilling captures, stories told.

In the twilight's gentle grace,
A tapestry of frozen space.
Through the cold, warmth interweaves,
In chilling light, the spirit leaves.

A Ballet of Snowflakes

Softly falling from the sky,
Snowflakes dance, they twirl and sigh.
Each one unique, a fleeting grace,
In this ballet, time finds its place.

Whirls of white in winter's air,
Delicate chaos everywhere.
Nature's waltz, a frigid whirl,
Embracing each soft, swirling pearl.

Gentle landings on the ground,
Silent beauty all around.
Winter's stage, a wondrous view,
In the hush, a dream come true.

Children laugh as they pause and stare,
Caught in wonder, hearts laid bare.
With outstretched arms, they join the play,
In this ballet, time gives way.

As night descends, the dance persists,
In the moonlight, magic twists.
Every snowflake tells a tale,
In winter's arms, we set our sail.

Resounding Echoes of Frosty Nights

In shadows deep, the cold winds call,
A whisper soft, a distant thrall.
The night unfolds with silver light,
And dreams take flight in silent night.

A frozen breath, a moment's pause,
The world holds still, as nature's laws.
Each star above, a glimmer bright,
Reflects the echoes, bathed in white.

Footprints trace in crusted snow,
Where secrets hide, and silence grows.
A symphony of frosty air,
Where haunting tunes drift everywhere.

The moon ignites the icy ground,
With every blink, a beauty found.
Resounding echoes fill the space,
Of frosty nights we once embraced.

Awake, we bask in crystal gleam,
With heartbeats soft, we dare to dream.
This tranquil night, a fleeting sight,
In echoes lost, an endless flight.

Frostbitten Fragments of Dreams

A shiver creeps through slumber's hold,
In fragments bright, our tales unfold.
The chill of night begets a sigh,
As dreams dissolve and gently fly.

Each breath a wisp of frosted dew,
Where whispered hopes find life anew.
The quiet chills our restless minds,
In frostbitten hues, the heart unwinds.

Reflections dance on windows' glare,
In shadows deep, we linger there.
With every pulse, the world awakes,
Unraveling paths our spirit takes.

We gather shards of night's embrace,
In frozen lines, we trace our space.
The warmth of thought, a gentle fire,
In frostbitten dreams, we soar higher.

Awake in wonder, we stand tall,
Beneath the stars, we heed the call.
In fragments found, our spirits reign,
In dreams of frost, we break the chain.

An Echo Through the Frosted Leaves

Whispers float on winter's breath,
Where nature's voice speaks of the depth.
In frosted leaves, the secrets lie,
Each echo tells a lullaby.

The stark embrace of trees so bare,
In silence deep, we pause and stare.
The melody, a gentle tease,
In whispers danced through frosted leaves.

A story cloaked in icy sheen,
Where every glimmer finds its scene.
Yet life persists in each small sound,
As echoes rise from frozen ground.

We wander forth in quiet sighs,
With every step, where beauty lies.
The world a canvas, painted slow,
In frozen art where soft winds blow.

Through bending branches, echoes sway,
In winter's grasp, we find our way.
The frosted leaves, a world so grand,
Where every whisper understands.

The Stillness Between Breaths

In quiet realms where moments pause,
A stillness fills without a cause.
Between each breath, we feel the weight,
Of silence dipped in softly fate.

The world outside fades quick and far,
In twilight hues, we find a star.
Each heartbeat laced in tranquil glow,
Where peace, like warmth, begins to flow.

No rush or hurry claims the hour,
In stillness found, we find our power.
With every sigh that fills the air,
The calm reveals our hidden flair.

Moments linger, time does bend,
In hushed repose, we start to mend.
The stillness calls, a gentle friend,
To hold us close until the end.

As night descends, we breathe anew,
In harmony, the skies turn blue.
The stillness sings, a soothing breath,
In whispers soft, we conquer death.

Murmurs of the Glacial Depths

Whispers low beneath the ice,
Secrets held in ancient vice.
Crystal echoes softly sound,
In the depths where dreams are found.

Glaciers hum a lullaby,
Beneath the vast and frozen sky.
Time stands still, a breathless dance,
In the silence, we find chance.

Shadows flicker, stories fade,
Memories in frost are laid.
Beneath the weight of frozen years,
Murmurs linger, woven fears.

Glistening shards of light cascade,
In this realm where time is laid.
Songs of ice and dreams entwine,
In the stillness, thoughts align.

With each crack, the voices wake,
Revelations that they make.
Chilling winds embrace the tales,
In glacial depths, truth prevails.

Carried on the Wind

Drifting softly through the trees,
Carried on the autumn breeze.
Whispers dance on fleeting sighs,
As the golden daylight flies.

Leaves take flight, a swirling sea,
In the air, they long to be.
Fleeting moments, songbirds call,
Lifting dreams, we rise and fall.

Winds of change, a gentle hand,
Guiding hearts across the land.
Voices linger, fade away,
Held in warmth of yesterday.

Through the valleys, over hills,
Echoes of forgotten thrills.
Softly sung, above the night,
Carried on, in endless flight.

Touch the sky, feel the embrace,
In the wind, we find our place.
Every whisper, every roam,
Carried on, we find our home.

Frozen Fragments

In the stillness, shards of light,
Frozen fragments, pure and bright.
Time encapsulated with care,
Moments caught in frozen air.

Crystalline dreams in icy lace,
Nature's art, a timeless grace.
Each reflection tells a tale,
Within the frost, echoes sail.

Snowflakes drift, a soft embrace,
Every pattern leaves a trace.
Fleeting forms of winter's breath,
Beauty found in stillness, death.

Chill of twilight, whispers call,
Frozen pieces, memories small.
In the quiet, silence speaks,
Hiding truths the heart still seeks.

Fragmented thoughts, icy yet clear,
In the winter's heart, we steer.
As the world slows down its pace,
Frozen fragments, time's embrace.

Tides of Winter's Whisper

On the shore where shadows play,
Tides of winter gently sway.
Whispers curl upon the sand,
In the chill, we take a stand.

Moonlit waves caress the night,
Carrying dreams within their flight.
Echoes soft, a haunting tune,
Underneath the silver moon.

Frosted air, a tender kiss,
Memories held in gentle bliss.
Where the sea meets winter's hand,
All is peaceful, wild, and grand.

In the depths, the cold wind bites,
Bringing with it whispered sights.
Tides retreat with every breath,
In their wake, we find our depth.

Seasons turn, yet still we hold,
Tides of winter, stories told.
With the ebb and flow, we learn,
In whispers soft, our hearts will yearn.

Serenity in the Shimmering Freeze

In quiet glades where snowflakes drift,
Soft whispers dance on winter's gift.
Beneath the stars, a crystal cloak,
Nature waits, as silence spoke.

Frozen lakes, like mirrors gleam,
Where shadows cast a gentle dream.
The air is crisp, serenity reigns,
In the hush of night, peace remains.

Moonlight bathes the slumbering trees,
Breath of winter, a soothing breeze.
Each flake a promise, pure and bright,
In the shimmering calm of night.

Softly draped in white's embrace,
Time meanders at its own pace.
Hearts unwind in the frozen grace,
Finding solace in this space.

Lost in the spell of winter's hand,
We stand united, hand in hand.
Beauty found in stillness grand,
Serenity shrouds this tranquil land.

Voices of the Cold Moon

Under the gaze of the solemn moon,
Whispers echo in a silver tune.
Frosted branches gently sway,
Calling forth the night's ballet.

Stars above begin to sigh,
As dreams take flight in the velvet sky.
A voice, though soft, carries far,
Guided by the northern star.

In the stillness, secrets weave,
Stories linger, hearts believe.
The chill draws near, but warmth ignites,
In the magic of winter nights.

Echoes of laughter, fading slow,
Footsteps crunch on the powdered snow.
The moonlight glistens as shadows play,
Voices linger till the break of day.

Through icy realms, the echoes flow,
In the heart, they ebb and grow.
Beneath the moon's enchanting light,
Joy is found in the quiet night.

When Silence Encounters the Frost

When silence meets the touch of frost,
Whispers of warmth are gently lost.
Nature pauses, holding breath,
The world enfolds in quiet depth.

Snowflakes fall like thoughts unspoken,
In the stillness, hearts are broken.
Yet in the chill, a beauty shines,
In frozen grace, where hope aligns.

Every flake a story told,
In icy patterns, dreams unfold.
Amidst the cold, a warmth ignites,
In the silence of winter nights.

Branches heavy with silver dew,
In their stillness, memories brew.
When silence walks, the heart complies,
Embracing peace where the frost lies.

Beyond the snow, a world awaits,
In quiet moments, fate dictates.
Each breath of winter, soft and clear,
Carries whispers for all to hear.

Glacial Dreams Adrift in Time

In the cradle of the icy night,
Glacial dreams take graceful flight.
Time unfolds like a frozen stream,
Carrying tales that softly gleam.

Amidst the chill, visions bloom,
Whispers linger, dispelling gloom.
Each breath a cloud, each heartbeat slow,
In the dance of the falling snow.

Frozen echoes of the past,
In this stillness, moments cast.
Drifting softly on winter's sigh,
Tracing paths where shadows lie.

Stars reflect in the frosted sheen,
As the heart stirs with what has been.
In icy grasp, the soul finds light,
In glacial dreams, the world's delight.

Time drifts on, a silent stream,
Under the spell of winter's dream.
Each falling flake a sacred rhyme,
In glacial dreams adrift in time.

Shadows Dancing in the Cold

In the moonlight, shadows play,
Whispers of night carry the sway.
Cold air bites with frosty breath,
Dancing figures, a tale of death.

Beneath the stars, they swirl and leap,
Secrets of winter, buried deep.
Silhouettes cast on the frozen ground,
In every silence, lost hopes are found.

A chill wind howls through trees so bare,
Lonely echoes fill the air.
Ghostly forms with every breeze,
They flicker and fade like leaves from trees.

Each step they take, a fleeting trace,
In the dark, they find their space.
Shadows waltz in cold embrace,
Under the blanket of night's grace.

As dawn approaches, they must part,
Echoes linger, a heavy heart.
In the day, their tale untold,
In shadows dancing, the night grows old.

Winter's Stillness Resounding

A hush has settled, the world sleeps tight,
Soft whispers of snow, pure and white.
Blankets of silence wrap the earth,
In winter's stillness, we find rebirth.

Frozen branches reach for the skies,
Underneath, the slumber of life lies.
Each flake that falls is a quiet sigh,
In the calm, dreams drift and fly.

The river, once noisy, now stands still,
Capturing moments, time to fill.
Ice encases the stories it weaves,
In whispers of winter, the heart believes.

Stars twinkle softly, high and bright,
Offering solace, a guiding light.
In the stillness, our spirits mend,
An embrace of winter, a quiet friend.

As dusk fades softly into dawn,
Nature's canvas, untouched, is drawn.
In winter's peace, we find our way,
In the stillness, we long to stay.

Songs of the Subzero Night

The night sings softly, a chilling tune,
Under the watch of a silver moon.
Frosted breath whispers through the trees,
A melody carried on wintry degrees.

In the depths of dark, the echoes play,
Each note a shiver that leads astray.
Voices of winter in harmony rise,
Like the snowflakes that dance from the skies.

A chorus of stillness, the world suspended,
In the subzero hush, all cares are blended.
Nature's lullaby, soft as a sigh,
Cradling dreams as they drift by.

With every gust that brushes past,
The songs of the night whisper, steadfast.
A symphony woven from ice and snow,
In the chill of the night, our spirits flow.

The stars become notes in a cosmic score,
Each twinkle a promise of something more.
We listen closely, hearts intertwined,
In songs of the night, our souls aligned.

Beneath the Layers of Ice

Frozen crystals bind the land,
Secrets hidden, frozen and planned.
Beneath the surface, life waits still,
In the heart of winter, dreams fulfill.

Beneath layers thick, the rivers flow,
Soft whispers tell of life below.
Silent beings, in slumber deep,
Resting gently, with secrets to keep.

Every creak of ice is a gentle call,
Echoes of life beneath the thrall.
In this stillness, stories unfold,
Of seasons past, of legends told.

The dance of frost paints the ground,
Nature's canvas, beauty profound.
Within the layers, hope remains bright,
Beneath the cold, there lies warm light.

As winter wanes and warm winds blow,
The icy veil will bid farewell, slow.
And as it melts, the world will rise,
From beneath the layers, life will surprise.

Reflections in a Icy Mirror

In the stillness of the night,
Moonlight dances on the lake,
Waves whisper secrets untold,
Shadows of dreams start to awake.

Frozen breath hangs in the air,
Each exhale a fleeting sigh,
Nature's canvas, cold and clear,
Underneath a silvery sky.

Trees wrapped in a crystal coat,
Branches glistening with frost,
Silent beauty, nature's note,
In this moment, not a cost.

Reflections shimmer on the ice,
Captured pieces of the soul,
Every heartbeat, every vice,
In the mirror, we are whole.

As dawn approaches, colors blend,
The icy surface starts to melt,
But memories will never end,
In frozen moments, love is felt.

Captured in January's Embrace

Cold winds whisper through bare trees,
January wraps the world tight,
A blanket of white, pure and soft,
In this cocoon, hearts take flight.

Footprints lead through glistening snow,
Every step a new path made,
Whispers of warmth in the chill,
A journey the cold has laid.

Fires crackle, embers glow,
Stories shared beside the flames,
Laughter dances on the air,
Remembering all the names.

With each flake that gently falls,
Nature writes a soft refrain,
Winter's touch, a lover's call,
Holding close through joy and pain.

Moments captured, frozen tight,
In January's tender grasp,
Each heartbeat, a flickering light,
As seasons change, we hold and clasp.

Beyond the Shatter of Ice

Beneath the surface, life does wait,
The ice may crack, but hope will rise,
In subtle shifts, we find our fate,
A world reborn, the sun will prize.

Shattered echoes, crystal sounds,
Nature's song in fragments play,
Beauty found in broken bounds,
Every dawn, a brand new day.

Streams awaken from their sleep,
Rushing forth with vibrant haste,
Memories from winter keep,
In the thaw, the past embraced.

Beyond the frost, the colors bloom,
Life's persistence, fierce and bold,
In the warmth, we shed our gloom,
As stories of renewal told.

Each step leads to paths unknown,
But onward we shall gently tread,
Through icy cracks, our spirits grown,
In the shatter, dreams are bred.

Echos from the Midnight Frost

In the silence of the night,
Whispers linger in the cold,
Stars like diamonds, shining bright,
Stories of the brave and bold.

Amongst the shadows, echoes creep,
Frosted breath of ancient lore,
In the calm where secrets sleep,
Midnight's magic, evermore.

The world is wrapped in silver light,
Each flake a tale that's long since spun,
In the chill, we find delight,
As echoes of our laughter run.

Time stands still in this embrace,
Moments carved in crystal dreams,
Every thought, a fleeting trace,
Underneath the moonlight beams.

So listen closely, hearts will hear,
The echoes of what once has been,
In the frost, our hopes appear,
Guiding us where love has seen.

Ethereal Ice

In the hush of a winter night,
Crystals dance beneath pale moonlight.
Silvery whispers fill the air,
Nature's magic, beyond compare.

Frosted branches, shimmering white,
Breathe the chill, hold on tight.
Glimmers of beauty, pure and rare,
A frozen world, beyond despair.

Each flake falls, a fleeting grace,
Bringing calm to the wildest space.
In the silence, dreams unite,
Ethereal ice, a beautiful sight.

Footprints echo on the ground,
In this peace, joy is found.
A canvas bright, nature's art,
Crafted softly, a work of heart.

Underneath the starlit skies,
Ethereal whispers of soft sighs,
Time stands still in frozen time,
Capturing moments, pure sublime.

Whispers Beneath the Surface

Beneath the calm of the lake's face,
Lies a world, a secret place.
Ripples carry tales untold,
In the depths, mysteries unfold.

Silence reigns, yet whispers flow,
Carried softly, a gentle glow.
Fish darting through shadows cast,
Echoes of wonders, unsurpassed.

Dancing reeds sway in a line,
Harmony sings, nature's design.
Life thrives in this hidden sphere,
Whispers echo, drawing near.

Light penetrates the azure deep,
Awakening dreams from their sleep.
Cascading sounds above the ground,
Whispers beneath, a song profound.

In stillness, beauty finds its voice,
In the silence, we rejoice.
A world where secrets softly play,
Whispers beneath, leading the way.

Crystalline Conversations

Glimmers spark in morning's light,
Crystalline wonders, pure and bright.
Each droplet holds a tale so true,
Conversations of the sky so blue.

Nature speaks in colors bold,
Stories of warmth, of love retold.
Leaves rustle with a gentle cheer,
Whispers of life, so rich and clear.

Snowflakes weave a blanket rare,
Softly falling, beyond compare.
Each one speaks in silence profound,
Crystalline conversations abound.

In the stillness, time stands stilled,
Nature's heart forever thrilled.
From earth to sky, in harmony,
Crystalline voices, wild and free.

In the twilight's fading hue,
Every shimmer tells of you.
Conversations flow, a symphony,
In the world's embrace, eternally.

Shadows in the Snow

Silent footsteps mark the ground,
In shadows lost, peace is found.
Whispers of winter drift on by,
Underneath the vast, gray sky.

Branches bare, their silhouettes,
Dot the white with soft regrets.
Memories linger, cold and slow,
Echoes dance in the falling snow.

Each layer holds a hidden tale,
Of laughter lost and the winter's wail.
In solitude, we find our grace,
Shadows whisper, time's embrace.

Frozen whispers brush the trees,
Carried softly on a breeze.
Within this world, so calm, so deep,
Shadows linger, secrets keep.

So let us walk this path of white,
And find our dreams in the quiet night.
In every step, a story flows,
In the magic of shadows in the snow.

Shimmering Silences

In twilight's soft embrace we dwell,
The hush of night begins to swell.
Stars whisper secrets, softly bright,
In shimmering silences, pure delight.

The moonlight dances on the stream,
Reflecting thoughts, a fleeting dream.
Each moment lingers, calm and sweet,
In the stillness, hearts can meet.

With every breath, the world aligns,
In quiet realms where love entwines.
A gentle touch, a soft-spoken word,
In shimmering silences, feelings stirred.

Echoes of laughter fill the air,
Soft shadows weave, a secret snare.
Underneath the canopy of night,
Shimmers of hope, a guiding light.

In moments cherished, we find our grace,
In shimmering silences, a sacred space.
Together we linger, lost in time,
As silence sings its tender rhyme.

Echoing Through the Chill

In frosty air, the echoes call,
A haunting tune that warms us all.
Each whisper resonates with pain,
Echoing through the chill, like rain.

The silver frost on branches gleams,
Carrying back our distant dreams.
Footprints carved in crystalline,
Echoing through the chill, divine.

As twilight falls, the shadows loom,
Nature wraps us in its gloom.
Yet in the dark, a spark ignites,
Echoing through the chill, warm lights.

Voices carried on the breeze,
A symphony of winter's freeze.
Each note, a memory we choose,
Echoing through the chill, it moves.

As seasons turn, the echoes stay,
A melody that won't decay.
In every heartbeat, hear the thrill,
Echoing through the chill, we will.

Icy Songs of Solitude

In snowy realms, the silence breathes,
Whispers wrapped in frosty wreaths.
The heart finds peace in the deep,
Icy songs of solitude, we keep.

Each flake that falls, a gentle sigh,
Painting the world as time slips by.
In the chill, we feel the calm,
Icy songs of solitude, a balm.

With every gust, the stories fly,
Adrift like clouds in an endless sky.
Reflecting dreams both lost and found,
Icy songs of solitude resound.

Alone we wander, yet never stray,
In solitude's arms, we learn to play.
Through frozen trails, our spirits roam,
Icy songs of solitude, our home.

So pause awhile, embrace the night,
In stillness, hear the world ignite.
Together, alone, we share this thrill,
Icy songs of solitude, hearts still.

Windswept Wishes

Beneath the sky, the wishes flow,
Carried on winds that gently blow.
We release them to the stars above,
Windswept wishes, dreams of love.

In every breeze, our hopes take flight,
Chasing horizons, seeking light.
Through valleys deep and mountains high,
Windswept wishes, touch the sky.

Each gust a promise, each sigh a prayer,
Carving pathways through the air.
With open hearts, we dare to trust,
Windswept wishes turning to dust.

In twilight's glow, the shadows play,
Fleeting moments slipping away.
Yet in our souls, their echoes cling,
Windswept wishes, forever sing.

So close your eyes and breathe it in,
Feel the whispers of where we've been.
With every breath, chase away the chill,
Windswept wishes on the hill.

Twilit Icicles

When the dusk hugs tight,
Icicles gleam in the light.
Shadows dance on the eaves,
Nature whispers, believes.

Fragile crystals they weave,
Stories of winter's reprieve.
Each droplet, a whispered tale,
In silence, they prevail.

Twilight wraps the cold air,
Catching dreams, unaware.
Time slows to a gentle sigh,
As the frosty stars pry.

Beneath the sky's embrace,
Icicles find their place.
In this still, frozen breath,
Life dances close to death.

The world is hushed and pale,
As winter weaves its veil.
In twilit moments, we feel,
A beauty that is real.

The Harmony of Hibernation

In the quiet, bears retreat,
Finding peace in their sleep.
Snow blankets the earth's face,
Time drapes a gentle grace.

Whispers of winds must wait,
As nature settles late.
Frost lingers on each tree,
A moment of harmony.

Stars twinkle in cold night,
Under skies, pure and bright.
In stillness, life remains,
Bound by soft, frosted chains.

Creatures tucked in their dens,
Dream of warmer trends.
Inside, rhythms unfold,
Tales of spring to be told.

The world rests, poised and calm,
As winter sings its psalm.
In hibernation's sweet grace,
Life finds a sacred space.

Vibrations of Stillness

Silent night, stars align,
In the stillness, we find.
Each breath an echo's tease,
Whispers dance with the breeze.

Frosted landscapes breathe low,
In shadows, secrets grow.
Nature pauses, aware,
In moments soft and rare.

Vibrations pulse through the cold,
Stories waiting to unfold.
Each flake a fleeting thought,
In silence, battles fought.

The heart beats in the freeze,
A melody that appease.
In the softest of sights,
Beauty blooms in the nights.

Stillness speaks without sound,
In this magic profound.
Within the hush, there lies,
Life's most tender surprise.

Echoing in Empyrean Ice

High above, the heavens glow,
In icy realms where dreams flow.
Echoes shimmer through the skies,
Mirrored in the cold, wise.

Crystal castles touch the seams,
Of fantasies and dreams.
Each echo, a gentle call,
Resonates in the ice's thrall.

Vastness holds a secret song,
Inviting all to belong.
In frozen halls, time suspends,
As the world beautifully bends.

In the silence, shadows play,
Carved in white, night and day.
Embrace the chill in each breath,
Life dances close to death.

Empyrean skies ignite,
With shimmering, frosty light.
Here, echoes find their grace,
In the glistening embrace.

Fragments of Frosted Time

In whispers cold, the moments freeze,
Each breath a sigh, a gentle tease.
The world stands still, as snowflakes fall,
In crystal dreams, we hear the call.

A clock that ticks with frozen hands,
Beneath the weight of winter's bands.
We chase the hours, lost in thought,
In sorrows sweet, the battles fought.

The dusk paints skies in muted hues,
As silence weaves, and time imbues.
Fragments glimmer, shards of light,
We gather 'round, igniting night.

With every flake, a memory spins,
A dance where loss and joy begins.
In frosted frames, we find our way,
Through fleeting dreams that winter sway.

And as the dawn greets crystal white,
We hold the past, embracing light.
In fragments found, our hearts align,
In frosted time, love's whispers shine.

The Lullaby of Ice

Softly sings the lullaby,
In icy notes where shadows lie.
Around the world, a subtle hush,
Where heartbeats blend, and memories brush.

The stars above begin to gleam,
In frozen dreams, we float and beam.
Each note a whisper, pure and bright,
Dancing softly, shattering night.

In the cradle of winter's sigh,
Time unfolds, we softly cry.
With every chill, our worries drift,
And in this space, our souls uplift.

Snowflakes twirl, a gentle twine,
In harmony, our spirits shine.
We close our eyes to feel the sway,
As ice's breath steers us away.

Embraced by night, we fade to dreams,
In silver pools where twilight beams.
The lullaby of ice, so sweet,
Carries us in its rhythmic beat.

Subzero Sentiments

Frozen hearts beat subtle tunes,
Underneath the silver moons.
Whispers travel through the chill,
As time unwinds, our dreams fulfill.

In quiet streets, the shadows play,
Where icy winds lead hearts astray.
We feel the pull of soft embraces,
In glacial realms, where hope traces.

Each frozen touch, a tale retold,
In moments pure, where we behold.
Subzero sentiments entwine,
With every tear, a glimmer twine.

In winter's grip, we find our muse,
As hearts ignite, no chance to lose.
With every breath, the frost ignites,
Lost in a world of twinkling lights.

We walk the paths of icy dreams,
Where love flows through the fragile seams.
In frozen echoes, we remain,
In subzero warmth, we'll rise again.

Timeless Resonance

In the silence, time stands still,
A whispered breath, a frozen thrill.
Through ages past, the echoes find,
The resonance of heart and mind.

With every gaze at distant stars,
We touch the void, erase the scars.
In timeless streams, our spirits soar,
We seek the light forevermore.

The chill wraps round like tender lace,
In every step, a warm embrace.
Resonance deep, where shadows blend,
In ageless realms, our souls transcend.

A tapestry of night displayed,
Embraced by frost, we are remade.
With each heartbeat, our dreams unite,
Defying boundaries of day and night.

In stillness held, forever free,
We write the lines of destiny.
In timelessness, our love will grow,
In echoes soft, forever flow.

Frosted Melodies

Whispers of the chilly breeze,
Dance upon the frosted trees.
Notes that shimmer in the light,
Crystals twinkle, pure and bright.

Echoes from the silent night,
Serenades of stars so white.
Snowflakes fall in soft embrace,
Nature's song, a quiet grace.

Gentle winds begin to swell,
Tales of winter's magic tell.
Hearts entwined in sweet delight,
Frosted dreams take flight tonight.

In the stillness, moments freeze,
Melodies that ride the breeze.
Harmony of winter's chill,
Softly echoes, lingering still.

With each breath, the world is new,
Frosted tones in shades of blue.
Whispered secrets, touch the soul,
In this beauty, we are whole.

Aria of the Arctic

Beneath the northern lights that gleam,
A world alive, a frozen dream.
Songs of ice and whispered air,
Nature's ballad, bold and rare.

Glistening plains of silver white,
Serenading stars at night.
Harmony in every flake,
A tranquil peace the cold can make.

Echoing through the vast expanse,
Silent notes in icy dance.
Polar winds that softly sing,
Winter's grip, a sacred ring.

Rivers freeze in crystal wraps,
Where echoes form melodic maps.
Each breath, a note upon the ground,
In this symphony, love is found.

Together with the snowflakes' fall,
Listen closely, hear the call.
An aria of love and light,
In the Arctic's endless night.

Ghosts of Winter's Breath

Shadows cast by pale moonlight,
Ghosts of winter, haunting sight.
Whispers linger in the air,
Memories of chilly nights laid bare.

Frosty fingers touch the ground,
Echoes of a silence found.
Frozen tales in icy streams,
Where time flows softly, chasing dreams.

Figures dance amid the snow,
Winter's breath, a soft hello.
With each gust, the past resounds,
A story in the silence found.

In the shadows, secrets keep,
Winter's ghosts in silence seep.
Chasing echoes, long ago,
In the frost, we seek to know.

Through the veil of icy mist,
Every sigh, a gentle twist.
Ghosts of winter call to me,
In their song, I feel so free.

Silent Symphonies

Underneath the silver sky,
Silent symphonies float by.
Notes of hush, a gentle thrum,
Nature's heartbeat, softly drum.

Each flake tells a tale untold,
Silent beauty, purest gold.
Winds of winter, soft and clear,
In this moment, all is near.

Harmony of earth and sky,
Winter's whispers, floating high.
Melodies in frosted air,
Sing of peace and tender care.

With the dawn, new notes arise,
Painting colors in the skies.
Every breath, a song to share,
In the stillness, love laid bare.

As the world begins to wake,
Silent echoes softly break.
In this symphony of light,
Hearts unite, embracing night.

A Solitary Thaw

In the hush of morning light,
A solitary drop takes flight,
Melting dreams of nights so cold,
Whispering tales that time has told.

Gentle warmth breaks winter's sigh,
Beneath the surface, hopes can lie,
Crystals fracturing, softly fade,
As spring begins its silent trade.

With every gleam of sunlit grace,
Snowy blankets find their place,
In soft surrender, they will lay,
To greet the dawn of brighter days.

Yet still, the chill holds onto past,
Hiding secrets in shadows cast,
Sprinkled still with winter's glow,
A fragile heart learns how to grow.

So let the thaw break through the frost,
Each moment cherished, never lost,
For in the warmth, the world will see,
The beauty born from what can be.

Murmurs of the Winter Croix

Whispers ride the icy breeze,
Rustling through the barren trees,
Murmurs echo, soft and low,
Tales of frost and moonlit snow.

In shadows cast by pale moonlight,
Figures dance in silvered night,
Elders speak of days long past,
Where frozen rivers flowed so fast.

Every flake that drifts and sways,
Holds a story from ancient days,
Frostbite kisses on frozen tongues,
Songs of nature, forever sung.

As twilight deepens into night,
Stars awaken, shining bright,
Secrets linger in the air,
Murmurs of the cold laid bare.

With every breath, a frozen sigh,
The world beneath a starry sky,
In winter's grasp, we find our place,
In the whispers, a warm embrace.

Fleeting Moments in the Frigid Air

Frigid air, a fleeting kiss,
Moments caught in winter's bliss,
Time suspended, sharp and clear,
Every breath, a crystal sheer.

Shadows stretch across the white,
Chasing echoes of daylight,
In the stillness, dreams take flight,
As silence hums its soft delight.

Patches of warmth, a fleeting glow,
Underneath the blankets of snow,
Each heartbeat sounds like thunder's roar,
In this chill, we seek for more.

Falling flakes, like whispered cheers,
Dance through days, then disappear,
Moments linger, then they flee,
In this winter's reverie.

Though the freeze may hold us tight,
In its grasp, we find our light,
For fleeting moments, sweet and rare,
Are treasures found in the frigid air.

Whispering Pines Beneath the Snow

Whispering pines, they stand so tall,
Draped in white like a gentle shawl,
Frozen leaves speak to the night,
Glistening softly in the light.

Beneath their boughs, the world seems still,
Each breath a promise, calm and chill,
Secrets held in winter's thrall,
Nature's silence, a sacred call.

Melodies carried on icy streams,
Whispers echo like distant dreams,
With every flake, a story spun,
Of warmth to come when winter's done.

Time expands beneath the frost,
In every moment, time is lost,
And yet, beneath the snow's embrace,
Life awaits, in hidden grace.

As dusk descends, their shadows dance,
In twilight's glow, the stars enhance,
Whispering pines, so wise and slow,
Guard their secrets beneath the snow.

Milton Keynes UK
Ingram Content Group UK Ltd.
UKHW010230111224
452348UK00011B/646